An Everyd

The Memoirs of a

Flying Officer
Kenneth Cockram
18.7.1921 - 7.6. 2013

ISBN: 978-1-326-83849-2

PublishNation
www.publishnation.co.uk

ACKNOWLEDGEMENTS

With grateful thanks to Ken's granddaughter, Rachel Tweats (nee Cockram), who transcribed his spoken words for these memoirs. She is currently a serving officer (Wg Cdr) in the RAF.

Also, for the invaluable contributions from Ken's children Michael, Elizabeth, Andrew and Richard.

PREFACE

In the months before he died, in June 2013 (at nearly 92 years of age), Dad was persuaded by several members of the family that he should record his childhood and war memories. As children we heard and became very familiar with his reminiscences of life in the RAF during his WW2 service and felt that these should not be 'lost' to the family.

Dad's detailed recollections, usually self-deprecating, often humorous, and always fascinating, remained undimmed by the passage of time and his advancing years. To hear Dad talk one might get the impression that no serious flying ever took place, but of course this was far from the whole truth, as life on the squadron was deadly serious most of the time! Many of his comrades were not as lucky as him and never returned home to tell their stories. Indeed Dad admitted, many years later, that for months after the War ended just the sound of a telephone would cause his heart to race (a telephone ringing usually heralded the call to 'scramble').

Although a very modest and unassuming man, we feel that our Dad epitomised the courage and spirit shown by so many people in the dark days of 1939 - 1945.

For us he was: *An Everyday Hero*

List of Contents

Chapter One:

1921-1941

I was born on the 18 Jul 1921 at number 68 Edward Street Parade, Ladywood, in Birmingham, the eldest son, of William Henry Cockram and Florence Gertrude Cockram, nee Davis. My earliest recollections are of lying in my pram and having people looking down at me and also of walking around the dining room at Erdington Hall Road, holding onto the table cloth as I was learning to walk. I also vividly remember being carried upstairs on 14 Nov 1924 by my Dad and shown my new baby brother, Tom, in bed with my Mum. I had a very happy childhood, my father and mother were very good parents indeed always doing their best although times were sometimes hard.

During the Great War 1914-1918 my Dad had been full time Assistant Secretary of the Birmingham Society of Sheet Metal Workers. At about the time of the general strike in 1926, someone else was appointed Secretary over his head, so Dad resigned. Unfortunately, due to his association with the Trades Unions, he was unable to get a job for about 2 years and was reduced to digging ditches for a living. He found this very degrading for a skilled man but I have always thought very highly of him for doing this. When he eventually got work, it was mainly in the motor trade in Coventry. Unfortunately, because of the depression, they only worked full-time for about 6 months, and then part time for the remaining 6-months of the year. Dad would never put up with short time working so he left to find full-time work around Birmingham. Because he was so skilled at his job, he usually wasn't out of work for more than a day or two but I never knew when I got home from school whether I would see him there with his tool box or not.

One night when he was coming home from Coventry, he was on the London to Birmingham express; as they approached Stechford Station, Dad stood up to put his coat on, the train lurched and he fell against the door; unfortunately, the door swung open and he fell out. Someone pulled the communication cord and the train was pulled into a siding whilst they sent a trolley back up the line with a stretcher to pick up Dad (or his remains). Much to their surprise, the rail workers met him walking along the line to meet them, without a scratch on him.

Some time before my brother Tom was born in 1924, we moved from Edward Street to Number 27 Erdington Hall Road in the suburbs, into a new terraced Council House (consisting of a lounge, dining room, kitchen, bathroom, 2 double bedrooms and 1 single). At first we had gas lighting but sometime towards the 1930s, we changed across to electricity which was a great help. I also remember that early on we didn't have toilet paper, everyone I knew used to use newspaper cut up into suitable sized sheets and strung together with string.

During the 1920's Dad used to make wireless sets for his friends and workmates. These required an aerial of about 20 to 30 feet in length slung from the eaves of a two storey house to a pole of an equivalent height. Valves had not yet been invented and a crystal & a cat's whisker were required to amplify the signal, but it was a very temperamental arrangement. When Dad went to install the set at the weekend we would all go along as well and frequently it required several hours of patient fiddling to get it working at all. Often we

2

would have to leave in the evening without having any success and Dad would have to go back later during the next week.

I remember sometime around 1930 my Grandmother had a visit from her doctor, Dr Trout, who turned up in an open horse-drawn carriage with a driver. The doctor was wearing a top hat and frock coat. I always thought that was most strange, for someone to appear to be that affluent, in an area of back to back houses and factories. At about the same time, I also remember my Grandmother taking me to see the first talking film that arrived at the Lyric Theatre, at the bottom of Edward St, it was called 'Rio Rita'.

I grew up playing around with some of the local boys on the road. When I was about 9 years of age, I remember I was out playing one evening with a boy from across the road, Dougie Wilcox, who was about a year younger than me. During our conversation I happened to mention the VC, and asked him if he knew what it was? He knew it was the Victoria Cross and said his Dad had one. I thought he didn't know what he was talking about and each went back indoors. I told my Dad that Dougie was stupid because he thought his dad had a VC; my Father said – "Yes he has!" It turns out that his father was Captain Albert Wilcox who had won the VC for destroying 3 machine gun nests single-handed when he was still a Lance-Corporal.

When I was 10 I won a scholarship to one of the local Grammar Schools and the scholarship fortunately included a maintenance grant to cover my expenses, such as books and uniform. I started at Central Secondary School, Suffolk Street, in the centre of Birmingham, in 1932. At sometime in the next few years they changed the name to Central Grammar School. I took my School Certificate examination for the first time in

1935 when I obtained 4 credits. This wasn't sufficient to enable me to go on to the sixth form so I stayed in the fifth form and retook the following year, achieving 8 credits, which took me to a Matriculation Certificate. Then in 1937 I went into the Sixth Form and I studied 3 main subjects: Mathematics, Physics and Biology; taking my Higher School Certificate in 1939 and obtaining a 'Pass' in Mathematics and Physics, and a 'Good' in Biology. I left school in July 1939, just prior to the outbreak of war. Just before leaving school, we had the opportunity to send a representative on a trip, organised and paid for by a Briton who had emigrated to Canada and set up a scheme, where boys from public schools in England and Wales could go for a month's trip to Canada, all expenses paid. The boy who was offered the chance to go was the Head Boy but he declined so we, the other five, cut cards for it and I won. I deliberated over it for a long time but as I was such a fussy eater I turned it down too, missing the opportunity to visit Canada.

In October 1939 I saw an advert in the paper for a position in the Secretarial and Accounts Department of Radiation Ltd a major holding company producing gas and electric cookers and fires and other apparatus. I applied for the position, got it and started on the following Monday morning. When I got home for lunch, my Mother said my Father had rung up to say that a position I had previously applied for as a laboratory assistant with the General Hospital in Birmingham had become vacant because the chap who had had the position had been a very firm supporter of Hitler and the Nazi party and when war broke out he had shot himself. The position hadn't been filled previously because the hospital had been evacuated due to the possibility of air raids; it wasn't known then how long it would be before they would appoint someone to take his place. However, the professor who had responsibility for the department had rung up my Father and said they were interviewing for the position and if I attended for selection the next day, I would definitely get the job but I had to attend for interview. As I had just started work at 'Radiation' on the Monday morning, I didn't feel I could leave the following day to go for interview for another job. I stayed with Radiation.

Whilst I was there the Home Guard was set up and I joined it and participated at the works at John Wright & Co, where the Radiation offices were situated. Whilst I was there I did several jobs such as dispatch rider (without anything to ride), machine gunner (without a machine gun) and various other stupid tasks they thought up from time to time. Mainly, we would do guard duty once a week around the factory. We would do 2 hours on and 4 hours off. I remember one night doing guard duty, I was there with a chap called Rolly, who was much older than myself; we looked around one of the air raid shelters in the main yard with our torches and saw a bundle of clothing on the bench. On closer inspection it turned out to be someone sleeping there. We didn't know who it was as one side of the factory ran alongside the railway embankment and it was easy for anyone to get onto the premises from the embankment. We woke the chap up and asked him for his identity card; he didn't have one but kept saying "you know me, you know me don't you". I said "I don't know you; you'd better come with me up to the guard room". We marched him off to the guard room on the first floor of the office building and as we got there, the Officer in Command of the Home Guard was coming out. He shone his torch on the chap's face and he said "Oh good God, it's the caretaker!" After that he got a lot of ribbing as he came around the factory. If our section of the Home Guard saw him they would shout out "where's your identity card?" which didn't please him very much.

One of the things we had to do in the Home Guard was to mount a ceremonial guard on a Spitfire which was on display adjacent to the Hall of Memory in Broad Street to solicit donations to buy a Spitfire. This was parked in a roped off square enclosure and we were stationed at each corner inside the enclosure, standing at ease and holding a rifle. Every few minutes we would shoulder arms and march around the enclosure a couple of times, before resuming our previous position. I was very amused when one woman, with a young boy, said to him "put a penny in the box and watch as the soldiers march round".

Things continued as normally as they could but in the first air raid on Birmingham, one of the very first set of bombs which fell hit the house opposite to us, partially demolishing it but fortunately we had no damage. In about March 1941 I was going off to work on morning on the tram and bumped into a friend of mine, Ralph Murphy, who told me he had just joined the RAF as a wireless mechanic and suggested I also joined because they had made an undertaking that when two friends joined up together they would remain together throughout their training. This sounded quite a good idea to me and I thought I might enjoy being a wireless mechanic so I broached the subject with my Mother and persuaded her to let me go and join the RAF rather than hanging around waiting to be called up and probably put in the infantry. So I went off to the recruiting office in Dale End and had the medical. I went in front of the Recruiting Officer who looked at my record. He said "I see that you are A1 medical – you'd like to be a pilot wouldn't you"? I said "Oh yes please" and that was that. That was how I joined the RAF – I didn't know how to go home and tell my Mother that I'd agreed to become a pilot but in the end she took it very well. A few days later I was called forward to

RAF Cardington to undergo further medicals to ascertain my suitability as a candidate for pilot training. I passed that OK and was inducted into the RAF on that basis. I fully expected to be sent straight off somewhere for training but was told that I wasn't immediately required and to return home until further notice. So I returned home and carried on at Radiation.

About the same time, Joyce Boyd and I started going out together. She was working in the same office as me. She was only 16 at the time and her parents weren't aware she was going out with anyone for a month or two. In July, she went with her parents to Deganwy in North Wales where her Father went into a recuperation home for a couple of weeks. I wrote to her whilst she was there and found out later that her Mother had intercepted the letter and knew all about us. My family went on holiday at the end of July into the beginning of August to Llandudno for a fortnight, although my Father was only there the first week as he had to return home. On the Monday morning we received a letter from him saying that I had passed my intermediate examinations for the Chartered Institute of Secretaries, which I had been studying for, over a couple of years, at night school in Birmingham. I had passed, with the exception of one subject but, with a special wartime dispensation, if I took the subject again the following Christmas, I would qualify as having passed the Intermediate Examination. So I said to my Mother, "well I'll do that then" but my Mother replied, "No you won't, you should have joined the RAF last Monday!". So my Father had phoned the recruiting office, told them the circumstances and they had agreed that I could return home and join the following Monday – 11th August 1941.

Chapter Two:

1941-1943 Flying Training

My deferred service came to an end and I reported for duty, on Monday 11th August 1941, to the Recruiting Office at Dale End, Birmingham. We were then marched to New Street Station to catch a train to London, to go to the Aircrew Reception Centre at Lord's Cricket Ground. Approximately half the intake who joined with me were policemen because, up until that time, the police had been a reserved occupation. But this was partly lifted to allow them to join the RAF, either as pilots or navigators.

We were billeted in flats in Regents Park Road and, over the next few days, were kitted out with uniforms and other necessities. Each day we were marched along to the restaurant at London Zoo for our meals.

On Saturday 20th August 1941 we were put on a train for Number 10 Initial Training Wing (ITW) at Scarborough. Here we were billeted in the Crown Hotel on top of the cliffs, above the Spa, facing the sea (Figure 1).

We did PT each day outside the hotel and then we were marched at a very quick pace, like light infantry (110 paces per minute), down to the Grand Hotel in the centre of Scarborough where we had lectures on various ground subjects. After we'd been there for about three weeks, we were told we were urgently needed abroad for flying training and we would be given 72 hours leave before embarkation.

I travelled home for the weekend and went for tea with Joyce's parents. Afterwards, we went to see the film 'Target for Tonight' at the Futurist Cinema – not a particularly good choice, considering the circumstances!

On returning to Scarborough, we were issued with tropical kit – so we knew it was unlikely we were going for training in Canada or the USA as I had anticipated.

On the 18th September 1941 we travelled to a transit camp at West Kirby on the Wirral Peninsular to await transportation to wherever we were bound. Whilst at West Kirby, and strictly against orders, we went into New Brighton one evening, to the fairground. After a ride on the dodgem cars I became aware that I no longer had my Rolex watch. On retracing our steps, I asked the attendant at the dodgem cars if anyone had handed in a watch. He said, "I don't know if you'd call this a watch," and he handed me the remains of a watch that had been squashed flat to about half its size.

On the 26th September we were put on the train from Liverpool to Gourock on the River Clyde, and then transferred by Lighter to the troopship 'HMT Empress of Russia', a Canadian Pacific liner, moored out in the centre of the river. When we got on board, I was astonished to find about 143 of us were expected to eat and sleep in hammocks or (for the lucky few) on a mattress on the floor, in an area about the size of a small church hall. There were eighteen of us at each table for meals and for slinging our hammocks at night.

One of the people at our table was a policeman called Pete Hodder, who I became friendly with because he'd been stationed at Victoria Road Police Station, close to where I'd been working in Birmingham. Pete was very much the Errol Flynn type, telling us constantly throughout the voyage that he intended to marry a Rhodesian girl whose father had a farm out there, and therefore he would be 'set up' after that.

In the section we were living in, which was on D-deck, just above the water line, there were three washbasins and three toilets; one of which was unserviceable for the whole voyage. In the toilet compartment there was usually water sloshing around – so if you wanted to use the toilet, when it was your turn you waited until the rolling of the boat sent the water away from the entrance, ran in, sat down, and hopefully lifted up your legs in time before the water sloshed back in!

The boat had been licensed to carry 898 passengers and crew, but there were 3,000 of us on board altogether. When we first saw where we were expected to stay, if we'd been anchored to the dockside we would've marched off again – to hell with the consequences! However, we didn't have that option and we soon got accustomed to it and settled into a routine. Actually, we very lucky compared to the Army Privates, as they were on decks as low as G-deck, in the bowels of the ship, and consequently they got very little fresh air – only what was funnelled in to them by big canvas scoops, and tubes fastened to the funnels of the ship. When we got into warmer climates it must have been very difficult for them down there between E and G decks; I can't even begin to imagine what their conditions must have been like.

On 4th November 1941 we arrived in Durban, where we were allowed ashore from early afternoon until midnight for the next two or three days. It was quite a transformation after wartime Britain and the troopship. First of all we had an excellent meal and then set about sampling the local "bevies" (alcoholic beverages). Our initial thought on the first evening was to visit a concert on the seafront that we saw advertised. Unfortunately, most of the 20,000 other troops who arrived on the convoy with us had the same idea, and we were unable to get anywhere near. So it was back to the bevies.

On the 7th November we were transferred to Imperial Forces Trans-shipment Camp (IFTC) Clairewood, just outside Durban. The camp was in three sections: Army in the middle; with the Military Police guarding the entrance; Navy personnel on the right hand side; and Air Force on the left. It was a very large camp because it was mainly used to put troops ashore on their way to the Far East. Troops would be there from one convoy and awaiting further troops, before being loaded onto ships to continue their journey. Quite rightly, it was thought that by the time the convoy arrived in Durban, the troops needed a break from troopship conditions.

Whilst at Clairewood, we were allowed out each day into Durban; but there was little to do other than eat and drink.

After two or three days, we were put on a train to Southern Rhodesia, now known as Zimbabwe. It was a comfortable journey that took about three days, and we took most of our meals on the train. But occasionally the train would stop at a station and all the passengers would alight, and go to the local hotel where our meal was provided. One such stop was at Mafeking, where most of the local inhabitants turned up at the station with their cars and took us RAF personnel around the town on a sightseeing tour.

We arrived at Bulawayo on 11th November and were put into Hillside Initial Training Camp (ITC). We did lectures on ground subjects and aerodynamics whilst we awaited transfer to flying school. Unfortunately there were about 600-700 of us in the camp and only four flying schools, which each took fifty pupils every six weeks. To make matters worse, if any Australians arrived, they were given precedence under a special arrangement with the Australian Government. So much for being needed **urgently** abroad for training!

When we arrived, it was the start of summer and the rainy season. We slept in huts with thatched roofs; and walls made of straw between two layers of whitewashed canvas that started about a foot above the floor and finished about two feet below the roof. There was a doorway at each end, but no door, and we slept about fifteen on each side of a central gangway, on straw palliasses [thin mattress bags, regularly stuffed with fresh straw], laid on blocks supported about a foot off the floor on bricks. (Figure 2)

We spent our first Christmas away in the camp, with a special Christmas dinner and some entertainment. It felt quite strange to have Christmas in such glorious weather.

On the troopship we had worn plimsolls to avoid damaging the decks but, when we arrived in Rhodesia, we reverted to our rubber-soled shoes. The ground was so hot that I developed a lot of blisters on my feet, which I covered with Elastoplasts – until one night I awoke with a severe pain all down one leg, and a lump in my groin. I went along to the sick bay to try to get some treatment, but it was in darkness. So I had to wait until the following morning, when I reported in sick. The Medical Officer examining me said, "You've got a poisoned leg. I've got two kinds of patients here, one with a scratch and another with his head hanging off – and you know which category you belong to!"

I was admitted to the sick quarters; and there my leg was covered in Ictholin (a black treacle-like substance) and cotton wool. It was very painful with my leg stretched out horizontally – even going to the toilet was agony – and it took about ten days before I was fully recovered.

The day came eventually, on 27th February 1942, when I was posted to Number 28 Elementary Flying Training School (EFTS), at Mount Hampden. There, on 2nd March 1942, I had my very first flight – in a Tiger Moth.

I flew with an instructor for about one hour each successive day, learning to take the plane off and land, doing medium and steep turns and recovering from spinning. This continued for a total of about 12½ hours with the same instructor. I then had two hours with another instructor, because I was having difficulty keeping straight on take-off and landing. As some of the other pupils were going solo after about seven hours of instruction, I was getting worried I wouldn't achieve the Chief Flying Instructor's test and might get 'canned'.

It was decided however that I was showing promise, and so I was transferred to Y-Flight (the flight for backward pupils) under Flying Officer (FO) Collins, who had done the flying for the George Formby film 'It's in the Air' – where George, who was ground staff, supposedly takes off by accident and ends up flying into a hangar.

FO Collins had a formidable reputation for not suffering fools gladly. But he was known to say that he could teach even his grandmother to fly - the difference being that we had only a limited time available to us. However, he usually succeeded, and his pupils were shielded from the Chief Flying Instructor's (CFI) test. I was reasonably happy about this. On the first flight with him he was as sweet as pie, and very complementary about everything I did. On each succeeding flight, however, he became extremely critical and bad-tempered and found fault with everything, for reasons that were unknown to me. I knew this was part of his method of instruction, but it got the better of me in the end.

Finally, on 21st March, after about three hours instruction that day, including innumerable take-offs and landings – and after I'd had a total of 18½ hours of instruction – we set off on another flight. After a further half-hour of criticism and derogatory remarks, he suddenly slammed the throttle shut on take-off and said, "You're going to finish up on a slab in a mortuary but you aren't going to take me with you!" And, with that, we taxied back to the dispersal area.

But, instead of getting out of the plane, he suddenly turned to me and said, "Would you like another chance?" Well, it was about the last thing I felt like but I still didn't want to be a failure so I said, "Yes." We took off again and only did a take-off, circuit and landing. After we'd taxied back to the dispersal area, he got out and said, "OK, off you go."

So came about my first solo flight, of 15 minutes, after 19¼ hours of instruction. When I got out of the aircraft, FO Collins was waiting and he said, "I was with the CFI in the control tower and I would like to congratulate you on a very nice landing."

It was felt I'd dropped so far behind that I wouldn't have time to complete the course - so I was sent back to Hillside Camp for six weeks, to await a transfer to the next course.

I returned to Mount Hampden with trepidation, wondering if the delay would've caused me further problems. But I started again with my original instructor with no further problems, and finished the course on 23rd July with a total of 89 hours in my log book – of which a total of 39 hours 40 mins had been flown solo, including 1 hour 25 mins being solo at night. (Figure 3). I was classified as 'above-average' as a pilot.

I was then posted to Number 20 Intermediate Flying Training School (IFTS) at Cranborne, Salisbury (the capital of Southern Rhodesia now known as Harare). I was to train as a fighter pilot on Harvard aircraft.

I think it was about this time that I was promoted to the rank of ASU (Acting Sergeant Unpaid). I did my first flight in a Harvard on the 5th August 1942. The Harvard was a single-engine low-wing monoplane, a two-seater with retractable undercarriage. On 19th October 1942 I was assessed by the CFI as an 'Average Pilot', and 'Above-Average' as a pilot/navigator. I ended the initial training course having completed 37 hours 10 mins solo daytime flying and 2 hours 35 mins of night flying, plus a further 42 hours with instructors – a total thus far, on Harvards, of 81 hours 45 minutes.

I was then moved onto the more advanced part of the course, Service Flying Training School – completing a further 50 hours 47 mins instruction – and finished my last flight at Cranborne on 12th June 1943.

Only one episode is worth repeating: which was when I was flying 'dual-instruction' and coming into land, and the instructor said, "I will take control." The Harvard has two fuel tanks, one in each wing. The fuel gauges to control the aircraft to take fuel from one tank to the other are on the floor at each side of the cockpit. As we were descending to the airfield, it crossed my mind that we always turned to a full tank for landing and so, noticing that the left-hand tank was empty, I switched to the other tank. No sooner had I done so than the engine started to cough and splutter as if it was going to cut out. Fortunately it occurred to me immediately that the instructor, who was in charge of the aircraft, had already turned to the full tank and I had turned it back to the empty tank. I hastily turned back to the full tank again and fortunately the engine picked up and we were able to land normally. When we'd put the aircraft away, the instructor said to me, "I don't know whether you noticed, but the engine spluttered on the approach and I thought it was going to cut out." I said, "Yes, I noticed that," but didn't tell him the reason. It was standard practice that the one flying the aircraft was strictly in complete control and I should never have touched anything!

When I finished my last flight, I was promoted to full Sergeant and awarded my pilot's 'Wings', backdated to 19th October (when I'd completed the Intermediate part of the course).

We left Cranbourne on 22nd January 1943, but were not told our final destination. However, on getting on the train to Durban, I was given a parcel by the local WVS containing, amongst other things, some woollies they'd knitted. We knew that if the knitwear was blue we were going back home, and if it was khaki we were destined for the Middle East. Only two were blue – one each for a Rhodesian and Jack Wagstaff, a

16

former policeman. On the train we picked up courses from other training schools at Gwelo and Bulawayo. Inquiring where the other policeman, Pete Hodder, was, they explained he'd married a local girl whose father owned a tobacco farm – just as he'd told us his intention was on the boat out to South Africa – and that he'd been held back as an instructor.

We arrived back at the transit camp again in Durban on 25th January 1943, and left on the 28th.

On our last day, there were four of us Sergeants who were detailed to keep order at the NAAFI canteen in the camp. The Orderly Officer came in at lunchtime and looked rather surprised to see us there drinking beer. He told us it was essential for us to be there when the canteen closed – so that we could escort him, with the evening's takings, down to the main part of the camp – because sometime previously an orderly officer had been attacked and the money stolen. We, on the other hand, were anxious to pay our last visit to Durban – which we did anyway. I often wonder how the orderly officer got on that night. Although I presume he was OK, as there were never any repercussions from our misdemeanour.

On 28th February 1943 we boarded His Majesty's Troopship (HMT) 'City of Paris' for the trip to Suez, arriving on 25th March 1943. I don't remember much detail of the accommodation, so it must have been better than on the voyage out to South Africa. The only thing I do remember was accidentally dropping my pipe overboard. So I changed over to cigarettes, which were much more convenient when we were having lectures. I never smoked a pipe again.

On arrival at Suez, we were billeted in Kasfareet Transit Camp – until 3rd April 1943, when we were transferred to

17

Number 73 OTU (Operational Training Unit) at Abu Suier near Ismailia, adjacent to the Suez Canal.

Initially we did some training flights on Harvard aircraft to re-familiarise ourselves after the long break since we last flew in January. After 16 hours 5 mins we converted to single seat Tomahawks (which I flew 33 hours 10 mins) and 3 hours 30 mins on Kittyhawks (which the Americans called Warhawks). Here we practised aerobatics, formation flying, dogfighting, air-to-ground firing & dive-bombing.

This course finished on 8th May 1943 and it was back to Number 22 Transit Camp at Almaza, Cairo, for nearly two weeks before we were transferred to Number 24 Transit Camp at Abukir – presumably to be nearer to Alexandria from where our next boat trip would depart.

We left on 23rd May 1943 to board His Majesty's Troopship (HMT) 'Egra', for a three-day trip up the Mediterranean to Tripoli in Libya, arriving on 29th May. I was then transferred via two transit camps (Numbers 38 and 39) to Zuara along the coast, about 40 km from Tripoli, near to the border with Tunisia.

Figure 1. Group photo at Scarborough
[Me - 2nd from the right on the 1st row]

Figure 2. Hillside Initial Training Camp - 'settling in'
[Me in the middle; Ted Collins on top!]

Figure 3. A Pilot at last

Chapter Three:

1943-1944 Operations

On 1st June 1943, I joined 239 Wing Training Flight at Zuara. It held pilots awaiting transfers to fill squadron vacancies.

239 Wing consisted of five squadrons flying American-made P40 Kittyhawks. They were Numbers 3 Sqn (RAAF), 112 Sqn (RAF), 250 Sqn (RAF), 260 Sqn (RAF) and 450 Sqn (RAAF). Also flying Kittyhawks was Number 5 Sqn (SAAF), of No. 7 Wing.

On 3rd June I was very pleased to be posted to [the now famous] 112 'Shark' Squadron – so named because they had adopted the decoration of a shark's mouth on the air intake below the front of the fuselage. (Figure 4)

The main difference we noticed on joining 112 Squadron was that there was one combined Mess for officers, including ground officers and the Non-Commissioned Officer (NCO) pilots, which was quite unusual but was designed to improve morale amongst the pilots. 112 Squadron was on rest after the conclusion of the North African Campaign and therefore June and July were taken up with practising formation flying; aerobatics and dog-fighting; air-to-ground firing; and dive-bombing. I flew 59 hours and 35 minutes. The weather was very hot so we spent most afternoons on the beach, and swimming in a small harbour with two wrecks for us to swim from and around.

Kittyhawks were fighter-bombers and evolved from carrying six anti-personnel bombs – three under each wing, weighing about 50lb each – to eventually carrying one 500lb bomb under each wing and either a 1000lb bomb under the fuselage or, when we occasionally went on a longer trip, a long-range fuel tank attached underneath the fuselage. On operations we usually flew at about 12,000ft and dive-bombed down to about 1,000ft or less. I found, in common with the rest of the pilots that, pulling out of the dive, I blacked out for 5-10 seconds due the effect of gravity forcing blood from my head down into my legs and feet.

One amusing incident whilst I was at Zuara was when Flying Officer Pepper, the equipment officer, sent two of the pilots to Tripoli with a three-ton lorry to pick up NAAFI supplies for the Mess. When they returned, they said they'd been given local brandy and, although the allocation was four bottles per man, they thought that that was excessive and had only brought two bottles per man. Pepper was furious with them and sent them back the next day to get the rest of the allocation – only to be told that the NAAFI had made a mistake and, instead of four bottles per man, it should have been one bottle for every four men! We didn't return any of them so it turned out very well in the end! Unfortunately the brandy was practically undrinkable; however, eggs could be obtained locally and we were supplied with condensed milk which, together with the help of an electric whisk on the bar, was turned into very acceptable eggnog.

The invasion of Sicily began on 10th July 1943, and the previous day the twelve most experienced pilots flew to Malta to take part in the invasion. There wasn't enough room for more people in the first instance, so some of us were held back for replacements as required. On 13th July the CO, Squadron Leader J. H. Norton, was shot down into the harbour at Augusta by an Italian Macchi 202 fighter. Two days later Squadron Leader Illingworth was appointed CO and remained with the squadron until the end of May 1944. Gradually, the remainder of the squadron's pilots flew over to Sicily as more landing facilities became available or as replacements were required.

On 31st July I flew a replacement aircraft, from Saulmon Landing Ground near Tripoli, to Bukino in Sicily. On 1st August I was ferried back to Casto Bunito near Tripoli, from Em Casabelia in Sicily, in a Douglas DC3 carrying battle casualties back to hospital in Libya. I then flew from Sualman Landing Ground to Agnone in Sicily and re-joined the Squadron at Bukino, a landing ground that had been carved out of a vineyard at the south-eastern tip of Sicily. Lying in our two-men pup tents, we could stretch out and pick grapes.

On Friday 13th August 1943, I did my first operational flight. Not a very auspicious date if I had been superstitious. Together with 260 Squadron we were tasked to bomb with a 2,000lb bomb barges evacuating German troops across the Straits of Messina to the toe of Italy. The Germans who were pulling out had lined up anti-aircraft guns on top of the cliffs on both sides of the Straits. One of my friends who I'd trained with, also on his first flight, went into the sea from 12,000ft having presumably been hit by ack-ack fire. Previously he'd always considered himself lucky, because he and another chap on the ground staff had volunteered to be aircrew whilst in Singapore and were posted away from there prior to the Japanese invasion. When we pulled out after bombing we flew along the Straits at low-level and had the anti-aircraft guns firing **down** upon us!

On 14th September we moved from Bukino to Agnone on the coast of Sicily, until the 20th September. Because 112 Squadron was part of the 'Tactical Air Force', we moved often, as the front line advanced – never more than 35-40 miles behind them. From Agnone we kept bombing shipping in the Straits of Messina until the 27th August when we flew Close Air Support (CAS) to Mitchell light bombers of the United States Air Force (USAF). The first night at Agnone we slept at sea-level but the mosquitoes were so numerous after dark that, despite anti-mosquito cream, for the rest of the time we moved to the top of the cliffs where we weren't bothered by them. In fact the Allies suffered more casualties from malaria than enemy action in Sicily.

On the top of the cliffs we had a small wooden hut, which had been used by the Italians for a field gun battery, as our Mess. There was a large gun and plenty of unused ammunition lying around so, as one of our pilots had transferred from the artillery, we decided to fire a few shells out to sea. The Group Captain visiting the Mess was inveigled into pulling a string which fired the gun. The Navy didn't think much of our antics and threatened to shoot back if we didn't desist, which we did immediately.

Three things of note happened whilst we were at Agnone.

First: the Medical Officers of the squadrons got together to find a solution to the effect on the airmen of being in contact with local women after being so long in the deserts of North Africa – and the consequent danger of contracting sexually transmitted disease. They eventually decided to engage two women and install them in a vacant farmhouse, with a Medical Orderly in charge to make sure everybody took the right precautions. It seemed to be very popular as, whenever we passed on our way to the landing strip, there was always a queue outside. However, Field Marshal Montgomery got to hear about it, and it was closed down again after only three days.

Second: the other preoccupation was beer, which had been almost non-existent in the desert. So, when Catania was recaptured, various teams were sent out foraging. They found a warehouse where an enterprising Sicilian had a lot of beer stashed away that the Germans had left behind. So all the beer was purchased and shared out amongst the five squadrons and divided equally between all of the personnel. The airmen on one of the Australian squadrons were told that the allocation was all that was available, and that when it was gone there would be no more to be obtained. However, they set to and finished off the whole allocation in short order. Because the officers and pilots had been more circumspect they still had some of their allocation left. The airmen, thinking the officers were holding out on them, asked for more to be shared with them. They were told they had been allocated their fair share and that no further supplies were available. That night the Officers' and Pilots' Mess, which was located in a building on Lentini Railway Station, was blown up. The CO was hopping mad and told the Station Warrant Officer to parade everyone at first light. The two of them were to search everyone's kit and anyone found with explosives was for the high jump. In the event, they found a stick of dynamite in everyone's kit so that ended the affair.

And third: whilst scavenging around Catania for beer, several of the 112 Squadron pilots found a warehouse containing several parts of aeroplanes. From papers found there, it turned out they were Caproni 100 aircraft (similar to Tiger Moths) belonging to the Catania Flying Club. On returning to base and mentioning it to the Group Commander, Jackie Darwin, he got each of the squadrons to send a lorry to 'liberate them'. When they were assembled there were seven complete aircraft. So each squadron had one, except 112 Squadron who got two, as we'd found them in the first place. They were used for flying around, sightseeing and giving trips to the ground staff. I took up one of the sergeants on 25th August for half an hour (Figure 5).

On 3rd September Italy signed a secret armistice and, after sending two aircraft to Ritali mid-way between Toranto and Brindisi, on 13th September we were the first Allied Squadron to enter Italy. We moved on 14th September to Ritali, ferrying some of the ground staff. Ritali had obviously, at one time, housed airships as there were very big tall hangars; although they were now only skeleton structures, presumably due to bombing.

On 15th September, five of us were detailed to fly to Salerno to assist with the landings there, because it was not going well and the only air support they had received was flown off an aircraft carrier. We were briefed on the situation by Group Captain Jackie Darwin who said that after taking off he would only do one circuit of the 'drome' to allow us to join him, and anyone who failed to do so or who returned with any ammunition in their guns would have to answer to him.

Jackie Darwin was quite a character. He'd been in the Café de Paris on the night it was bombed. His wife had been killed in his arms and consequently he had a pathological hatred of the Germans and wanted to retaliate to the utmost degree.

At first light on 16th September, Jackie Darwin and his Number 2 took off together first. Unfortunately, Ritali was a grass strip with very light, dusty, sandy soil and their take-off raised a cloud of dust. Normally this would've made it impossible for anyone else to take off for another 15 to 20 minutes. But, in view of his strictures the night before, the next two took off successfully and then Dave Brown and I took off with me as his Number 2. We couldn't see anything in front of us so, consequently, I don't think we got lined up properly on the runway. When I'd got my tail up I came out of the cloud of dust to find I was travelling diagonally across a rough field at the side of the runway, heading for some trees about 100 yards away. By this time I was doing about 70mph; but not enough to get off the ground. Rather than for my own safety, I was concerned that there were airmen from one of the other squadrons sleeping in tents among the trees. I therefore tried shutting down the throttle and selecting the landing gear 'up', in the hope that the aircraft would drop onto its belly. But, although the two bombs were pulled from the fuselage of the aircraft, it didn't drop down and I hit the first tree with the port wing, which sheered off next to the fuselage. This had the effect of swinging the aircraft round counter-clockwise. It carried on and the fuselage hit the next tree and was cut in half before the aircraft came to a halt. I'd been well strapped-in, so suffered no injuries and was helped out of the cockpit by airmen in the nearby tents – to find there was nothing of the plane left behind me except a sheet of amour plating! Our two flight commanders had been watching the take-off and turned up to find out what'd happened. I heard one say to the other, "We'll have to get him into the air again as soon as possible." I can honestly say that it didn't really affect me to any extent, and I flew a normal operation again in the afternoon.

In the 24th September we moved up the east coast to Bari. On 26th and 30th September I flew two missions. During the first we struck Motor Transport (MT) and a tank, without opposition. Rifle and machine gun fire was always a problem during strafing as it couldn't be seen but it only needed one bullet to hit the engine cooling system and drain it and the engine would seize up in about 15 minutes which, if you were well behind the German lines, was a bit of bad luck! On the second trip we also bombed and strafed MT and a tank, in spite of plenty of accurate 88mm anti-aircraft fire.

Whilst at Bari we had a day off operations and, after a lift into town, had a good look round.

We were billeted in a farmhouse and had rigged up a shower outside made of a bucket of water suspended on a frame, with a rope to tip it into a tin with holes in it. It was quite effective. Whilst here we also had tent sidewalls erected as a screen and two buckets with wooden seats for toilets. There was one bucket in one corner, and another one in the opposite corner. I found it quite embarrassing sitting there facing the CO!

In the month of September, I flew on 15 operational missions totalling 24 hrs 5 minutes and then, on 3rd October, we moved from Bari to Foggia Main aerodrome, which had been the headquarters of the Italian Air Force. It comprised quite a lot of blocks of flats in the town, which were completely deserted. We took advantage of the situation to liberate a radiogram with a pile of records, and a three-piece suite for our Mess – whilst a small Fiat car was taken by the CO as his own personal transport. After 3 days however, the Military Police (MPs) moved in and put notices up around the town, saying that anyone found looting would be liable to be shot on sight. This didn't deter a bunch of Australians and they were caught in a block of flats which were then surrounded by MPs who marched them out one by one – only to find the first two out were both Padres – so they all got away with it!

On 7th October 1943 Group Captain Jackie Darwin was killed on a mission with 260 Squadron. He was hit by anti-aircraft fire and flew into a hillside. His Number 2, whom he had strictly instructed before take-off to "follow him whatever happened", unfortunately took him at his word and also flew into the hillside and was killed.

On 27th October we moved from Foggia Main aerodrome to Melini close by, to make room for heavy bombers to use the long runways. In October I flew for thirteen hours on nine missions, including two over Yugoslavia. It involved flying an hour each way over the Adriatic – which was not nice, in case we should have engine trouble or suffer from enemy action and have to ditch in the sea [Adriatic].

In November I only flew one mission of 50 minutes, as I'd had a bad cough for about three weeks. In the end I had to report sick to avoid having to fly. The Medical Officer listened to the bubbling in my chest and immediately put me in the squadron ambulance. It took me to a field hospital, which was entirely under canvas. They put me to bed in one of the tents and I had five doctors come and listen to my chest during that afternoon. By that time I was getting a bit nervous. However, one of the doctors said not to worry, they were just intrigued because of the noises in my chest which were interesting and unusual. After 2-3 days in bed and keeping warm, I was feeling much better. But they decided to put me on a course of the new wonder drug M&B 693, with which Winston Churchill had been treated for pneumonia. That had the effect of making me feel worse than ever, as I was hallucinating during the daytime. After a couple of days of having what seemed like nightmares without being asleep, I palmed the rest of the tablets and threw them down the loo. I was discharged from the hospital after about two weeks and told that I'd had unresolved pneumonia. They wanted to send me to North Africa to recuperate in a warmer, drier climate – but I wouldn't go, because I didn't want to leave the squadron, and I thought it a possibility I might be posted to the Far East where they were also flying Kittyhawks. Several of my friends came to visit me in hospital and told me I'd received a parcel, of 200 Senior Service cigarettes, from home. "Where are they then," I asked. "Oh, we smoked them," they replied. Who needs enemies when you've got friends like that?

At the beginning of November, the Equipment Officer who was in charge of our Mess went to the CO [Commanding Officer] and told him that, unless we did something about it, we would have nothing to drink at Christmas. The CO therefore authorised him to take a three-ton lorry with a driver, and cash of about £600 that we'd collected with a whip-round. He was to go to the Naples area. The CO thought it would take him a day to get there, a day to get some liquor, and a day to return – so three days approximately. But when he didn't return for a fortnight, the CO was hopping mad, until he explained that he'd arranged with the owner of a pensione on the seafront at Naples, to take three or four of the pilots at a time, for four to five days 'Rest and Recuperation', because no-one had had any leave for some time. He'd also requisitioned accommodation at the hot springs in Herculaneum as a 'Leave Centre' for the airmen [non-commissioned ranks].

Because I'd just returned from hospital, I was one of the first to go, together with two of our Aussie pilots and a driver. We drew supplies from the NAAFI and handed them to the proprietor to cook for us, and we swapped a bottle of Irish Whiskey with him for a bottle of Apricot Brandy, which was much more acceptable. One afternoon we went to the Other-Ranks Rest Centre at Herculaneum, because the Equipment Officer had said he'd arranged for a bus load of girls from Naples University to come to a dance. When we got there we were not impressed, as we got the impression that the girls had actually attended the 'University of the Streets'!

It was rumoured that, if arrangements were made with the proprietor, he would 'obtain' some girls. Accordingly, the two Aussies arranged to each have a girl brought-in on our last night and they would have the evening meal with us. We'd just sat down to eat when who should walk in but the Padre, who explained he was on his way to the Other-Ranks Rest Centre at Herculaneum but, as the journey had taken him longer than he expected, and there was a curfew from 7pm in Naples, he'd decided to stay the night at our pensione. He quickly sized up the situation and, because you could not tell he was a parson, except by two small badges on his collar, one of the girls decided he looked better than the Aussie and she tried to make up to him. The meal eventually finished and we all went to our rooms (the girls accompanying the Aussies). I hadn't been in my room for more than a few minutes before one of the Aussies asked to speak to the proprietor, as the girls wanted more money than they [the Aussies] had been told, and I was the only one that had been able to converse with the proprietor.

He spoke a little French and I did my best with my schoolboy French. We got the matter settled in the end and all retired for the night.

Sometime later, after we'd returned to the Squadron, the Padre (who alternated between all the squadrons on the Wing) came to us for a few days. He tackled me in the Mess one evening and, referring to the situation in Naples, apologised for any embarrassment that he'd caused us by turning up unexpectedly. He said, "I don't know if you noticed that one of the girls was making up to me." I said that I did, and he said, "I was very tempted, you know!"

After a week or two at Mileni Landing Ground we moved. We'd had a lot of rain and it was impossible to move transport around the aerodrome, because it was all deep mud. So we moved to Celoni Landing Ground, which was just a short distance away but had not been affected.

On the 20th December we were tasked to attack gun positions in the front line at Ripa near Chievi, where the Germans were holding strong defences between the sea and the 35 miles or so of the Apennine Mountains which rose to about 13,000ft. When we got over the target we were subject to what I call in my log book, "Intense light, medium and heavy anti-aircraft fire;" and Bob Wilkinson, with whom I had shared a tent in Sicily, was hit at low-level pulling out after bombing. Immediately his aircraft burst into flames. Bob pulled it up to about 700ft and baled out. We later found out that he'd landed safely and was made a Prisoner of War. I later met him at Church Fenton in 1946, when he told me about the experience – including how he'd jumped from the lorry taking him away from the front line, only to be recaptured and given a good hiding for his trouble.

My aircraft was hit by what I think was a 20mm tracer shell, which I saw coming up all the way from the ground. It made a hole, measuring about a foot across, in the port wing root (Figure 6).

It made the aircraft very difficult to control and I had to brace the control column with my left knee to stop the aircraft rolling to the left. The shell had obviously damaged the controls in some way and had also stopped my air speed indicator from working. It took me about 20 minutes to get back to the vicinity of the aerodrome, with me wondering all the way how I was going to land – not knowing the speed, and also whether the shell had affected the flaps and the undercarriage. Whilst this was all going through my head I'd been gradually losing height and I saw the runway at Meleni, which we'd evacuated, straight ahead. So I decided to go for it instead. In the event, I landed without too much difficulty, but the Engineering Officer was a bit put out at having to retrieve the aircraft. I felt that in the circumstances, I'd got out of the situation very well, so I wasn't at all worried.

On 31st December, we again bombed gun positions at Ripa – again against heavy opposition. One of our South African pilots was shot down and ditched in the sea, but was picked up and returned to the Squadron six days later. In December, I'd flown 14 operational missions, taking 17 hours.

January 1944 was a busy month. We made ten trips to Yugoslavia on anti-shipping strikes off the coast near Spit and the Islands near Korcula. During January I flew 17 missions covering a total of 26 hours and 55 minutes.

On 29th January we moved to Cutella Landing Ground, near Vasto on the East Coast. The landing strip had been laid on the sands, with Pieced Steel Planking (PSP). Each piece was 10ft long and 1ft wide, with piano-type hinges that were slotted together with steel rods. When it rained, which it did quite often, the sand drained away leaving hollows. The mobile crane was driven onto the runway to lift sections of the planking so that more sand could be shovelled underneath to level-up the runway. The runway was very short, about 900 yards long, which was OK for taking off but left a lot to be desired on landing. There were one or two instances of aircraft overshooting and tipping up on their noses in the sand. The solution was to put two 40 gallon oil drums, painted white, on either side of the runway, a short distance from the start of the runway, followed by another pair painted red a little further along. It was desirable to touch down before the white drums, but if you hadn't touched down before the red drums it was obligatory to go around.

At Cutella, our Mess was a Nissan hut, with a large tent next door to eat in. We painted the inside of the hut pale blue with the dope used on the underside of the aircraft. As the weather was quite cold, someone had the bright idea of making a heater out of a 40 gallon oil drum. A small opening flap was cut out at one side, about six inches from the bottom, and a chimney was made from tins in which the butter came, with a hole cut in the roof for the chimney. Aircraft fuel was supplied from a long-range tank outside. A small-bore tube came from the tank, along under the floor, and came up about six inches above the floor. There was about two inches of water placed in the bottom of the oil drum and, when the tap on the long-range tank was slightly opened, petrol would drip onto the water and spread out. When a match was popped through the flap, the petrol burned and heated us very efficiently during the cold weather.

A rather amusing incident occurred one evening in the Mess when some of the more senior people were playing Bridge at one end of the hut by the bar. Our 'liberated' radiogram was in the middle of the hut and most people were either reading or in conversation. A record of Gloria Jean singing a very catchy tune called 'the Penguin Song' besotted one of the sergeant-pilots, an Aussie by the name of Bernie Peters. Unfortunately, on this evening he overdid it and was about to play it for the umpteenth time, when one of the Flight Commanders who was playing Bridge, suddenly got to his feet as Bernie was about to play the record again and said, "Bernie, if you put that record on again I'll break it!" Bernie said, "You wouldn't dare," and put the record on again; at which the Flight Commander stormed over and grabbed the record and threw it onto the floor where it broke in two. The rest of the evening there was a very subdued atmosphere in the Mess. Having a Pilots' Mess with Officers and NCOs together, it was an unwritten law not to pull rank in the Mess. The next morning a note was put up on the Mess notice board by the Flight Commander, apologising for his actions the night before.

In the evening we were all in the Mess, with the Bridge school in full swing, when all of a sudden outburst Gloria Jean and the Penguin Song again. Everything came to a stop as we wondered how on earth Bernie had managed to get another copy of the record in the middle of nowhere. When we listened more closely, however, you could hear 'click, click'. Bernie had stuck the two pieces of the record together. It didn't last the complete song but long enough for everyone to be in fits of laughter, including the offended Flight Lieutenant. It proved to be the catalyst for a very good party for the rest of the evening. It was small events like this that helped to take some of the stress out of operations.

In February 1944 I flew on seven operational missions for a total of 9 hours 35 minutes – including three trips to Yugoslavia and one to Monte Casino (although we didn't drop our bombs due to 10/10 cloud cover). Whilst at Cutella, we often had targets in the central part of Italy. This necessitated crossing the Apennine Mountains, which rose to over 13,000ft. We used to fly through a col [a cutting in the mountains] that was about 35 miles away. On taking off from the coast we had a continuous climb to reach the col, at about 12,000ft – which, with a full bomb load was just about possible. Several times on these trips I thought we wouldn't make it, but we always did.

On the 3rd April we were tasked to bomb the Town Hall at Macerata which intelligence believed was a Fascist Headquarters, and it was thought that a high-level meeting of Fascists and Germans was taking place. In 1996 Bert Horden, who'd been on the raid, was invited back to Macerata, where a ceremony was taking place in remembrance of the operation. He was told that there had, in fact, been no such meeting taking place, but it was thought that the raid had been planned to allow the escape of a British Intelligence Officer and a group of Partisans, about to be executed. There were only two Germans killed, but 93 civilian casualties.

During April I flew on 19 operational sorties, totalling 33 hours and 35 minutes – predominantly against railway bridges and in close support to the Army. It was during this time that we developed the system of Forward Air Controllers, by stationing one of our senior pilots in the front line with the Army, equipped with a radio for contact. If the Army had a heavily defended area that they wanted us to bomb, they would give us the map coordinates and, on reaching the target, the Forward Air Controller was able to direct us in to the target more accurately, and also to tell us to adjust our aim more precisely.

Towards the end of May, the weather was getting warmer and we hadn't used our patent heater in the Mess for some time. One evening I was sitting on the sofa with Flight Sergeant Nordstrand, a New Zealander, both of us having had our meal in the tent next door. The majority of the remaining pilots were still having their meal, all except the CO and a few of his cronies from the other squadrons. Suddenly Nordstrand said to me, "There's a strong smell of petrol here. I'll bet some silly so and so has turned on the tap on the long-range tank, I'll go and check." He came back in and said it had been turned on but he'd turned it off again. After a few minutes sitting, he said, "Isn't that smell of petrol overpowering, why don't you light it?" I replied, "You're joking!" He said, "No, go on, light it." So I struck a match and threw it in through the flap near the bottom. The result was instantaneous: a 6ft flame shot out towards Nordstrand; I've never seen anyone leap over the back of a settee the way he did! There must have been more petrol than we'd anticipated because, before long, the 40 gallon drum was getting red-hot, the makeshift chimney was bent here-and-there and looked in danger of breaking, the wooden struts between the two corrugated iron sheets making up the Nissan Hut started to char, and for several feet around the chimney the aircraft dope started to burn and give-off a lot of smoke. Eventually Nordstrand and I thought it advisable to leave the hut. When we got outside, there was an audience of about 200 airmen, from several squadrons, watching as flames about 6ft high were shooting out of the chimney. Shortly afterwards, the CO and his companions staggered out. They'd been up the other end of the hut at the bar, and hadn't noticed what was happening until they were smoked out. Unbelievably, as far as I'm aware, there were no repercussions from the incident.

Whilst we were at Cutella, we heard about the Dambusters raid on the Mohne and Eder Dams. Our Group Commander, a South African Colonel (not knowing the elaborate and lengthy preparations they'd needed to make, to successfully breach those dams) decided to bomb a dam – at the foot of the Apennine Mountains and behind the German front line – with the hope of flooding the entire area between there and the sea. Accordingly he led a raid, leading 260 Squadron, with us [112 Sqn] bombing second. The Group Commander's Number 2 scored a direct hit on the dam, but of course it failed to do any serious damage.

On 3rd May six of us, accompanied by two spitfires, and after bombing a railway viaduct, saw a group of aircraft totalling at least eighteen, flying at about the same height as us and going in the opposite direction. They turned towards us and, at first, I thought they were probably Americans. But then they turned in behind us and started firing. Our Flight Commander told us to make for the deck and head for home, an instruction which appalled me as this was only the second time we had run into enemy aircraft and, as fighters, I thought that (although out-numbered) we should've had a go at them. On a personal level also, as my Number 2 and I were still trying to join up with the flight after bombing, and were still quite some way short of our flight and about 500ft lower, I thought that his order had in effect thrown us to the wolves! Anyway, I could see that a large number of them had lined up behind me and were firing at us. I knew we couldn't outrun them and so I chose the standard defence of turning in to meet them. When I came out of the turn I saw a Messerschmitt 109 passing just in front of me, turning right to left, firing cannon shells out of his red propeller spinner (although he hadn't a hope of hitting me from that position), with a Focke-Wulf 190 behind him as his Number 2. Fearing I was so close that I was about to run into one or other of them, I flipped over to the right, behind them, and dived steeply to the deck before pulling up again. I was expecting to be in the middle of them and having to 'mix it'. Imagine my surprise when I got back up to about 3,000ft and looked around – to find not a sign of an aircraft anywhere in the sky. My Number 2, Lieutenant M. White (SAAF), had had to decide whether to follow me (as was his duty), or whether to follow the Flight Commander's instructions. Unfortunately he took the latter course. I heard him call over the RT that he'd got a lot of them behind him, and I heard no more from him; but he was shot down and killed! I'm convinced that if he'd followed me, he would have survived as I did.

May was quite a busy month and, on 22nd May, we flew from Cutella Landing Ground to Sant Angelo Landing Ground.

In June I flew on six operational missions for a total of 8 hours 50 minutes, finishing my tour of operations on 5th June when six of us, led by Flight Sergeant Peters, bombed and strafed motor transport (MT) on the road north of Orvinio. Unfortunately, for some completely unexplained reason, Sergeant Tickner, who had only joined the squadron on 6 May, broke away from the formation at about 10,000ft and slowly, in a descending spiral, hit the ground and exploded – although we called him frantically over the RT, but without effect. We also lost Lieutenant Churchill (SAAF) who was, however, made a Prisoner of War.

When we got back to the aerodrome the CO, Squadron Leader Aherne, who was an Australian, turned to Flight Sergeant Peters, who was also Australian, and said, "That's it Bernie, your tour's expired." However, since Bernie had only done 196 hours of operations, he had no alternative but to tell me that I was also tour-expired (because I'd done 198 hours 30 minutes) rather than be accused of favouritism. Accordingly, I left the squadron on 27th June 1944, having completed 129 operational missions. During that time we'd lost a total of 24 pilots: 14 having been killed; 9 made Prisoner of War; and our CO who was shot down over Yugoslavia, but was picked up by the partisans and returned to the squadron five days later – although by this time he'd already been replaced.

I went from the Squadron to a transit camp in Naples to wait for a boat to take me back to Egypt, although I had hoped to be returned home.

Figure 4.

Figure 5. A 'liberated' Caproni plane

Figure 6. Damage to wing

Chapter Four:

Egypt and Palestine

On 17th July 1944 I embarked on HM Troopship (HMT) 'MV Batary', which arrived in Alexandria on 22nd July.

I was put in No.22 Personnel Trans-shipment Camp Almaza, in Heliopolis, Cairo to await a posting. I fully expected to be posted as an instructor to an Operational Training Unit (OTU), flying American [P47] Thunderbolts.

However, on 8th August I was posted to No.26 Anti-Aircraft Cooperation Unit (AACU), stationed at El Firdan on the banks of the Suez Canal, about three miles north of Ismailia. Here I was flying [British] Hawker Hurricanes – doing dummy attacks and search-light cooperation at Port Said, and Heliopolis near Cairo. I found flying the Hurricane very easy, because it was very stable and had no obvious faults. The unit also flew American Baltimore twin-engine light bombers, towing 'drogues' (which were like windsocks) for live-firing targets.

I was at El Firdan until 6th September when I was posted to No.26 AACU Detachment at Maryut Airfield, Alexandria. The airfield had been constructed on the salt marshes on the outskirts of Alexandria and consisted of asphalt runways and concrete parking blocks for the aircraft. There was a canal running around three sides of the aerodrome with a pumping station at each corner, pumping water back into the salt marsh to keep the aerodrome stabilised. On one occasion whilst I was there, a crowd of local native navvies were resurfacing the runways and were using a tar boiler about the size of a steamroller to provide the material. One night they were foolish enough to leave the tar boiler standing in the salt area – only to find next morning that it had sunk through the salt surface and completely disappeared!

Maryut had only very meagre facilities, but at least it had the attraction of being able to sample the nightlife in Alexandria. I stayed at Maryut until 30th January 1945, when I was posted back to El Firdan.

At Maryut we flew for the Naval Gunnery School and became very friendly with the instructors at the school, who were all Petty Officers and had been boy entrants into the Navy. The Petty Officers' Mess at the Naval Barracks was run by the members as if it were a ship at sea and the instructors we knew, being permanently stationed there, held all the official positions in the club. A party of us were invited there to be shown around and we enjoyed typical Navy hospitality with plenty of rum. Apparently everyone in the Mess was entitled to a tot of rum each day, but some of the younger and more transient members didn't take up their allocation and the gunnery school instructors were able to take advantage of this; so the rum was freely available to them and their guests. Whilst at Maryut, the Navy decided to close down the Petty Officers' Mess as a self-run club and transfer it to the NAAFI. The instructors were incensed at the decision, as they'd built up quite substantial funds that would all be transferred to the NAAFI. To avoid this, they threw a big party for 400 people, to which we were invited. On arrival, we were given tickets for a number of drinks but when one of our instructor friends saw us he said, "Give me your tickets, you won't need those!" and so we didn't. We were invited into their locker room from time to time, where they produced bottles of rum to augment the beer on general offer, and we had one of the most memorable parties I have ever attended!

Also whilst I was at Maryut, another of the pilots was a Warrant Officer Bursey. Bursey had been very friendly with a girl in Glasgow; but her father didn't approve of him and had put a stop to the friendship. However, fate stepped in and, after joining the WRENs, she'd been posted to Alexandria – where they'd met up again and become friendly to the point where they decided to get married, getting permission from the authorities to do so. Bursey asked me to be his Best Man. So I attended the wedding and the wedding breakfast at the Fleet Club in Alexandria. The bride's friend, also in the WRENs, was the bridesmaid and, because the wedding took place on a Saturday, I was at a loose end on the Sunday; so I invited the bridesmaid out. I was very amused on arrival at the 'WRENery' to have to sign for her, as presumably the Navy took very good care of the girls in their care. We had a meal and a pleasant evening at the Fleet Club, and I delivered her back safely afterwards.

We passed a very enjoyable Christmas (Figure 7) at Maryut (although the weather was cold and wet), and stayed until 30th January 1945 when I was posted back to El Firdan.

At El Firdan we flew from 5.30 in the morning until 1 o'clock in the afternoon, after which it became too hot. So we had every afternoon and evening off, from about 2 o'clock onwards.

I soon became friendly with an Australian pilot, Warrant Officer Collier, and also the Flight Sergeant in charge of the Instrument Section, who had both become members of the Yacht Club at RAF Ismailia (a pre-war RAF Station). They spent each afternoon at the Yacht Club on Lake Tunisia, a part of the Suez Canal. As outside members, not being stationed at RAF Ismailia, they found it very difficult to obtain a yacht for their use and had therefore to make their own. At El Firdan, in addition to No.26 AACU there was also No.108 Maintenance

Unit (MU). It received aeroplanes, disassembled and shipped over from the USA in wooden crates [for re-assembly]. So consequently there was plenty of timber available for their use. For sails they used drogue fabric which, when washed to get rid of the stiffening agents and pink colouring, and dried in the sun, became very similar to poplin and was very popular for being made locally into pyjamas (and sails). So popular in fact that one day it was noticed that they were short of something like over 200 drogues. A Court of Inquiry was set up to establish the cause of the shortage, but I never heard what conclusion they came to. It should never have reached that stage since they could have written off any number having been shot away during target practice. Anyway, having their own boat made them very independent and they kindly invited me to join them most afternoons. After a very exciting time yachting, we were able to use the Yacht Club facilities to enjoy afternoon tea – usually brown bread and prawns.

On 13th February I'd returned from flying for the Army at Port Said at about one o'clock to be asked by the Flight Commander if I'd ever flown a Fairchild Argus – a small, high wing monoplane with a four-seater cabin. "No," I told him, "but why do you want to know?" At first he said, "It doesn't matter," but when I pressed him he said that our CO's Fairchild had been blown loose of its moorings the previous day and overturned, crumpling one of the wings. They had, however, found a replacement at Aboukir, on the coast near Alexandria, and needed a pilot to fly it back to El Firdan. He said that Warrant Officer Collier, who had a lot of experience flying Fairchilds, would fly someone up in the Fairchild belonging to the CO of No.108 Maintenance Unit to bring back the replacement aircraft. I immediately volunteered and, after some hesitation, because he couldn't find anyone else who did have experience, he agreed to me going. He said, however, that I should be most careful and make sure I followed Collier's instructions. On 15th February we took off in the early afternoon, together with a friend of ours, an air gunner who usually acted as a drogue operator on Baltimores. It was a very ropey take-off and, after we reached a safe height, I turned to Collier and told him I didn't think much of his take-off. He said that he thought it was not bad for a first attempt! When I said that the Flight Commander had told me that he [Collier] had a lot of experience on Fairchilds, he just laughed. I should say that it was very unusual to meet an Australian Warrant Officer pilot, as they would usually, at that time, be commissioned straight away. However, Collier had been in the RAAF pre-war as an officer, but had been cashiered and dismissed from the Service for low flying over a lake in an Anson and blowing over several yachts in his slipstream. At the outbreak of war he'd been allowed to re-join because of the shortage of pilots; but of course he would never be granted another commission.

We had a very uneventful journey to Aboukir, lasting about two hours, and reported to the Duty Pilot on arrival, telling him we'd come to collect a spare Fairchild. He told us it was all ready for us but was short of fuel to get us back to El Firdan and, because they didn't have any of the correct type of fuel there, we would have to fly to Alexandria, about fifteen minutes away, to refuel. We did this but, after we'd been refueled, it was getting late in the afternoon. So I told the Duty Pilot it was going to be dark by the time we got back to El Firdan. "Oh, it'll be alright," he said, "They're night flying at Ismailia tonight and the flare path will be on." I told him I wasn't at all happy at the thought of having to land the Fairchild at night, because it would be only my second landing in a Fairchild, to which he agreed. So we left the planes there and went into Alexandria to spend the night. There we met a bunch of submariners with whom we had a very good evening. So much so, that we promised to take them for a flight the next morning and they promised to give us a trip in their submarine! These visits never took place of course, but we headed off back to El Firdan. We met a very annoyed Flight Commander, who knew he'd been taken for a ride – but knew he couldn't do anything about it, when I told him that I didn't think he would have wanted me to risk a night landing in Ismailia in the CO's personal plane.

Shortly thereafter I was promoted to Warrant Officer and, being in this rank for a while, another pilot suggested to me that we both apply for a commission, which we did and both were accepted. We were given a few days leave in Cairo and Alexandria – where we had our new uniforms made – and then returned to the Officers' Mess at El Firdan; having made the transformation (in my case) from 1425541 Warrant Officer K. Cockram to 191882 Pilot Officer K. Cockram. It felt quite strange at first, to move from the Sergeants' Mess to the Officers' Mess on the same Station, but we didn't find any awkwardness and soon settled in.

On 9th April 1945 I was posted to No.26 AACU Detachment at Ramat David, near Haifa, in Palestine; and was flown there as a passenger in a Baltimore.

Ramat David was built on land leased from a Kibbutz and we used the main road through the Kibbutz every day to get from our living quarters to the aerodrome. This gave me my first opportunity to see girls for the first time in 'hot pants' – for all the good it did me! However, we did get to participate in a tour of the kibbutz to see how they organised their lives on a communal basis. This included seeing them fighting with staves, because they were not allowed to have firearms – but were preparing for the time when the British left and they knew they would have to defend themselves against the Arabs. The Arabs, who did most of the menial jobs around the RAF Camp, regaled us with the bloodthirsty things they had in store for the Jews.

I was flying Hurricanes at Ramat David at first. But, on 14th June 1945, I flew a Spitfire V for the first time, and continued flying them for the remainder of my time at Ramat David.

On one occasion, several of us were invited to a party at an Army Officers' Mess at Acre, some way down the coast from Haifa. Returning quite late at night, we were stopped just outside Haifa, by an Army Private standing in the road and flagging us down. He explained that he'd run over an Arab in his lorry; and a large hostile crowd had gathered and were intent on lynching him. He was obviously terrified and begged us to stay with him until the Military Police arrived. This we did, and passed about a quarter of an hour or so in great trepidation – because it looked as though, if anything happened, we would undoubtedly suffer the same fate as him! Fortunately, a detachment of Military Police arrived before the situation got out of hand and we gladly handed over responsibility to them.

Whilst at Ramat David, I heard that Hugh Kelly, my Cousin Edna's husband, was in the RAF and stationed at El Shameel, south of Haifa. So I got permission to fly over there to visit him. I heard later that, before they were married, Hugh, being an Irishman, had intended to leave Birmingham and return to Ireland to avoid being called-up. Auntie Nell, who was Edna's mother, told him that if her daughter wasn't good enough to fight for, then he wasn't good enough to marry her, so he stayed and found himself in Palestine. After the war I reminded him of this visit, but he professed not to remember it.

On 11th September 1945 I flew from Ramat David to Deversoir in the Suez Canal Zone, where the unit had been moved to from El Firdan. I flew again on 14th September for the last time with No.26 AACU, before being transferred to No.26 Personnel Transit Camp, Kasfareet near Suez – prior to commencing my journey home at the completion of my overseas tour.

We were taken to Alexandria and embarked in a troopship there. We sailed along the Mediterranean, destined for Marseille in the south of France having made one short stop in Grand Harbour, Valetta, Malta to pick up two Navy types, who were also returning to the UK.

We spent a couple of days in a transit camp near Marseille, before being put on a train across France to Dieppe – a journey of about 24 hours in very primitive conditions! It was October and seemed very cold to me after being in semi-tropical conditions for four years. The compartment on the train comprised wooden seating with no upholstery and overnight I slept up on the netting of the baggage rack. We had no eating facilities on the train, and had to eat our meals standing up in a siding.

On reaching Dieppe we spent a night in a transit camp, before being put on a boat sailing to Newhaven.

Before leaving Egypt we'd been told to take only the minimum of luggage with us, because we would have to carry everything ourselves as we were transferred from one part of our journey to the next. I was amazed to see one of our party, in addition to his kit bag or suitcase, also had a large old-fashioned trunk. It turned out to be full of liquor. He didn't have any difficulty in getting help to carry it, as everyone was tickled by the idea. When we landed at Newhaven we were led into a large customs shed and told to put our luggage on the bench. I was so interested to see how he got on because we'd been told we would each only be allowed to have two bottles of liquor and 200 cigarettes. So I stood near him, and he put the trunk unopened on the bench. When the Customs Officer got to him he tapped the trunk and asked, "What've you got in there?"… "Oh it's full of liquor," the Serviceman said. The

Customs Officer gave a laugh, marked it with a cross in chalk, and said, "Off you go then."

We caught the train to the same transit camp at West Kirby in Merseyside that we'd left from four years earlier.

The next day, 19th October 1945, Trafalgar Day, I got on a train to New Street Station, Birmingham – where I was met by Joyce, my mother and father, and by my brother Tom.

Figure 7. Christmas 1944 at Maryut

Chapter Five:

UK until Demobilisation

In October 1945, I had four weeks' disembarkation leave. During that time Joyce and I got engaged to be married, and Tom had his 21st birthday party.

I was then summoned to Fighter Command Headquarters in London for a posting.

When I got there, the only flying job they could offer me was with a Spitfire Squadron at Wick in Scotland. I said, "I'm not going to Wick, I've only just got back from four years overseas, and Wick's a damn sight further away than the Middle East!" The chap I was talking to suggested that the only other thing they could offer me was as a GCI Controller. I said, "What's that?" and he said, "It's 'Ground Control Intercept' Controller, using radar – but I don't know if they'll accept you, what's your demob number?" I told him it was number 39, and he said, "Well, you might just scrape in."

He gave me the name of an officer to go and see. Well, I don't think the chappie had seen anyone for a while, because he jumped at the chance of me becoming a Controller and told me to go straight to a course that was starting in Trimley Heath near Felixtowe. I told him I hadn't come prepared to go straight away; I'd just come to find out what my posting was (I'd taken the precaution of leaving all my kit in the Guard Room). So he let me go home for the night, and told me to travel down in the morning.

The next day I travelled by train down to London and then across London to Liverpool Street Station. I then caught another train to Ipswich, before getting a bus to Trimley Heath. When I got there, I found that although they had been stationed in billets in the village, they'd already moved into RAF Martlesham, which had recently been vacated by the Americans. Nobody else had turned up for the course yet so it didn't start straight away. I said I could easily go back home again but they told me I'd better wait until the weekend. It was Wednesday so I kicked my heels until Friday when I travelled back home. It was a complicated journey, and even more so returning on a Sunday night. I had to get a train from Birmingham New Street Station at 8 o'clock at night, which was already overcrowded and difficult to get on. I travelled to Euston and then crossed to Liverpool Street Station to get the last train out to Ipswich. It left at two in the morning and was full of drunken Yanks. When I got to Ipswich I found myself out in the cold and waiting for a bus, alone.

Following the course, I was stationed [in the Mess] at RAF Church Fenton in Yorkshire, and worked at No.12 Group Operations Room at Tadcaster. After doing a shift there one morning, I returned to Church Fenton to be told that the Orderly Room had been trying to get in touch with me all morning.

On reporting to the Orderly Room, I was told that a posting had come through for me from Air Ministry Headquarters in London. "Where to?" I enquired, and was told it was to RAF Sledge Green. "Where's that?" I asked. Only to be told, "We don't know – it's on the Secret List!" So I said, "Well, how on earth do I get there then?" They offered, "We think it's near Pershore in Worcestershire; we suggest you go there and enquire at RAF Defford." That suited me very well [because Worcestershire is very near Birmingham]and my fiancée, and my parents, lived in Birmingham. So I hastily packed and went back home for the night.

The next morning I caught the train to Pershore. I then rang RAF Defford and said to the operator, "I've been posted to RAF Sledge Green, can you help me please?"…"Oh, I don't know anything about it," she replied. "Well, what do you suggest I do?" I said. 'Where are you?" she asked and, when I told her I was at Pershore Railway Station, she suggested I got the bus out to Defford to see the Adjutant.

On arrival at RAF Defford, I went to the Adjutant's office and, when I explained my predicament, he said, "The CO of Sledge Green sometimes comes in here on a Tuesday or a Thursday. I suggest you go and get some lunch in the Mess. If he comes in, I'll tell him you're here."

At about 4 o'clock, a chap came up to me [in the Mess lounge], addressed me by name, and said, "Come with me." We went outside, got into a small RAF Hillman Minx van, and headed out into the countryside. By this time I was almost too afraid to ask any questions, particularly as he was wearing an RAF officer's greatcoat, from which all badges of rank had been removed, and no hat. However, eventually I plucked up courage and asked him where we were going, because nobody would tell me anything. "Oh!" he said, "Sledge Green is near Bredon Hill. I'm the CO and I'm a civilian, and so are half the personnel there. But there are about 25 of you RAF chaps on the unit, under the command of a Flight Lieutenant, and you're all billeted in the Abbey Hotel, Malvern."

It turned out that the unit was tasked to arrange for aircraft to be flown, by RAF Defford, for targeting by the Radar Research and Development Establishment at Malvern when testing their equipment. We were responsible for the direction of the aircraft during RADAR testing trials, and for their safe return to Defford in the event that the boffins forgot all about the aircraft whilst attending to a malfunction of their precious equipment under trial!

After four continuous years' overseas, Sledge Green proved to be a very welcome posting, near to my home, until I was demobbed.

I was demobbed on 5thJune 1946, at RAF Uxbridge near London.

During my five and a half years in the RAF, I flew for a total of 806 hours 20 minutes, of which 689 hours and 5 minutes were solo and 117 Hours 15 minutes were dual with an instructor. I also flew as a passenger for about 13 hours altogether, in a Baltimore, a DC3 Dakota and an Avro Anson.

Appendix 1

Figure 1: Flying Officer Ken Cockram Flying Hours by Aircraft Type

Aircraft Type	Total Hours	Dual Hours	Solo Hours
Tiger Moth	89:00	49:00	39:40
Harvard	176:35	67:55	108:40
Tomahawk	33:10		33:10
Kitty Hawk	240:15		240:15
Caprioni 100	1:10		1:10
Mustang	1:00		1:00
Argus Fairchild	5:40		5:40
Hurricane	221:45		221:45
Spitfire	37:45		37:45
Total Flying Hours	**806:20**	106:55	699:25

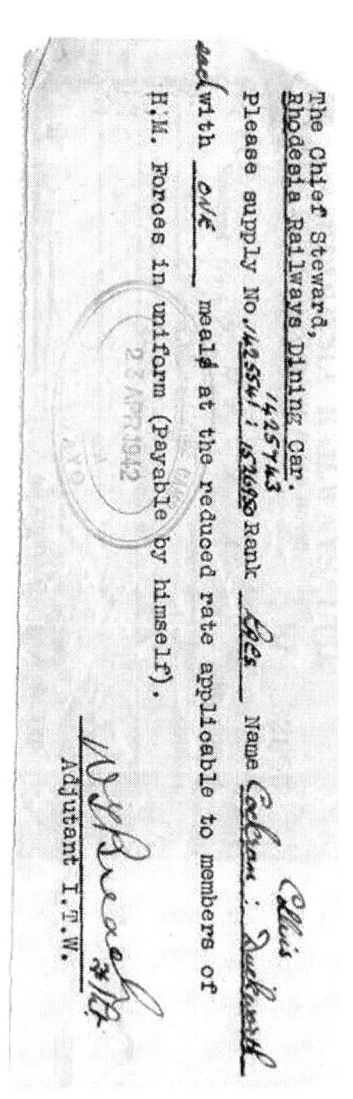

Figure 2: Rhodesian Railways receipt

58

Appendix 2

August 1946	Rejoined *Radiation Limited*
April 1947	Married Joyce Boyd
	Trained and qualified as a Certified Accountant (becoming a Fellow in January 1980)
January 1962	Joined *John R. Woodvine & Son Limited*, Shrewsbury, as Company Secretary and Accountant
	In the following years, through takeovers and acquisitions, *Woodvine & Son* became first *William Asquith & Son*; later *Norton Grinding Machines*; and finally *Warner Swayse Limited* of Ohio, USA, for whom Ken continued as Local Director of Finance and Personnel
1972	Ken accepted the "Queens Award to Industry" from HM Queen Elizabeth II on behalf of the Company in a ceremony held at Buckingham Palace

December 1976	Shrewsbury factory closed by parent company. Having already moved to live in Churchstoke, Powys, Ken accepted the position of Chief Accountant of *Churchstoke Hatcheries Limited*, part of the *Vestey Group*
August 1988	Shortly after his retirement Ken & Joyce moved to Stourport-on-Severn to be closer to their family, where he became an active member of Droitwich Aircrew Association
June 2013	Ken passed away

Printed in Great Britain
by Amazon